# *Colorado's*
# Hidden Wonders

## Photography & Text by Grant Collier

Collier Publishing
Lakewood, CO

# About the Author

Grant Collier has been working as a professional photographer since 1996. His images have been featured in magazines throughout the United States and Europe and he is the author of the books *Colorado: Yesterday & Today* and *Colorado: Moments in Time.* He also produces a yearly wall calendar and many of his images are available as posters and fine art prints. More information on Collier and his photography can be found on the web at: http://www.gcollier.com.

©2006 Collier Publishing
http://www.collierpublishing.com

Text and photography © Grant Collier.
Cover & text design by Grant Collier.

ISBN 0-9769218-2-0
Printed in China.

# Foreword

After completing my books *Colorado: Yesterday & Today* and *Colorado: Moments in Time*, I believed I had seen the vast majority of Colorado's diverse landscapes. I had traveled through every county in the state and had revisited the most spectacular regions several times. Therefore, while taking photos for this book, I was surprised to discover numerous hidden gems in Colorado that I was previously unfamiliar with. Some of these places are so little known that they have remained largely untouched since American explorers first set foot in Colorado over two hundred years ago.

The sublime solitude of these wild places created a dilemma for me because if a place receives too much publicity it could cease to be a hidden wonder. I have therefore chosen not to reveal the names or specific locations of some of the most remote and fragile places I have photographed. This book is therefore not intended as a guide book. It is intended to bring a unique portrait of Colorado to those who love and appreciate solitude and beauty but do not have time to thoroughly explore the state's manifold landscapes. For those who do want to personally experience some of Colorado's hidden wonders, my advice is to simply travel off the beaten path. You will be amazed at what you can discover with a little patience and perseverance.

Grant Collier
Lakewood, CO

# Introduction

After climbing Longs Peak in 1873, the intrepid world traveler Isabella Bird wrote:

> I was uplifted above a world of love, hate and storms of passion,
> for I was calm amidst the eternal silences, bathing in the living blue.
> For peace rested that one bright day on the mountaintop.

Today, climbers on Longs Peak may not find the eternal silences that so enthralled Bird, for each year nearly 20,000 people attempt to reach the summit. Nevertheless, Colorado still harbors remnants of the primordial lands that Isabella Bird encountered in her travels over a century ago. These places often lie at the end of difficult jeep trails or are tucked away in remote wilderness areas. Some of these lands are rarely ever serrated by the faint contours of human footsteps, while others are so immense that people are given the illusion of being entirely alone. Occasionally, these hidden wonders are located surprisingly close to major roads and highways but have remained largely unknown while thousands of travelers pass by on their way to national parks and other attractions.

While these lands can be found in nearly every corner of the state, there are a few that merit special attention due to their unique geology and spectacular scenery. One such place is Wheeler Geologic Area in southern Colorado. Wheeler contains a labyrinth of otherworldly hoodoos, pinnacles, and domes. These features were carved out of a layer of volcanic tuff, which was deposited approximately 28 million years ago during a period of exceptional volcanic activity throughout the state.

Due to its impressive rock formations, Wheeler was proclaimed a national monument by Theodore Roosevelt in 1908. However, the area was so remote and inaccessible that the monument was abolished in 1950 and control was turned over to the National Forest Service. Although Wheeler has begun to see more visitors in recent times, it remains one of the least-visited natural wonders in Colorado. Today it can only be accessed by way of a long and difficult jeep trail, followed by a short, but steep hike.

Another hidden gem in Colorado is a remote canyon on the Western Slope that contains the second largest concentration of natural arches in the world. Like Wheeler, it is only accessible by way of a long, rugged jeep trail and a moderate hike. The jeep trail can become impassible when wet and the area can be unbearably hot in the summer. As a result, it is little wonder that this canyon receives so few visitors each year.

Those who do make the journey to this area are rewarded with an impressive array of arches, from small windows to immense sandstone openings. These arches were carved out of Entrada Sandstone, the same sandstone that produced the formations in Arches

National Park.  Unlike most arches in that park, which were formed out of sandstone fins, the arches in this area were carved out from the rim of the canyon.  Rain and snowmelt gradually eroded the rock along the side or top of the canyon into an alcove, cave, or pothole.  As these openings grew larger, they eventually carved a hole through the canyon rim, thereby creating a natural arch.

One other geologic oddity lies in a hidden canyon on the eastern plains of Colorado.  This area, which is surrounded by endless miles of rolling plains, contains a wonderland of pink, orange, and purple rocks.  Some of these rock formations have eroded into the shape of giant mushrooms, giving a hiker the feel of visiting a surreal, fictional landscape.

Like the volcanic rocks at Wheeler and the natural arches in western Colorado, these rock formations in eastern Colorado were formed by the erosive forces of water.  Summer rains and winter snowmelt have carved out a small canyon and exposed layers of colorful clay, which were deposited fifty to sixty million years ago.  This clay is capped by resilient, white sandstone, which has prevented the softer sediments below from completely eroding away.

Archeologists believe that Native Americans first discovered these multihued rock formations approximately 9,000 years ago.  These early inhabitants are thought to have used the abundant quantities of colorful clay to make paint.  They may have also used the area as hunting grounds, as bison bones have been discovered in the vicinity.

While the above-mentioned wonders have special value because of their unique geology, they represent only a few of the thousands of hidden marvels located throughout the state.  Each of these places offers a glimpse of nature in its purest and most primal form.  They provide an escape to a raw and elemental existence that is rare in modern society but which our ancestors confronted on a daily basis.  When visiting these lands, one can almost hear the echo of distant voices from ages past.

While these lands offer a window to the past, they can also provide a glimpse into the future.  In recent years, some once-forgotten lands have been overrun by development, mining, and drilling, while others are threatened by such endeavors.  Although these activities can cause irreparable damage to the landscape, there is promise that much of Colorado's unspoiled scenery can be preserved.  Many of Colorado's hidden wonders have been protected by the federal government, while others are designated as wilderness study areas.  Only time will tell if the efforts of those who have worked to protect these lands will produce a lasting testament to the "eternal silences" of the once wild and untamed West.

Indian paintbrush, sunflowers, and American bistort fill a valley below a spectacular waterfall in a remote part of the San Juan Mountains.

A small waterfall along the Elk River flows between granite rocks near the Mount Zirkel Wilderness in northern Colorado.

The Roaring Fork River surges through sculpted
rock formations near the Grottos of Aspen.

Erosive forces have carved rock formations into otherworldly forms in a secluded part of the Western Slope.

An escarpment of colorful rocks makes up part of a fascinating hillside resembling Bryce Canyon in Utah.

Sunflowers, Indian paintbrush, and purple daisies thrive
below Fletcher Mountain in Mayflower Gulch.

Fall colors provide added beauty to a spectacular, but seldom-visited waterfall in the San Juan Mountains.

The last light of the day illuminates Cinnamon Mountain near the town of Crested Butte.

An ancient, wind-swept bristlecone pine stands in a timeless pose atop Windy Ridge as fog rolls into the valley below.

The jagged rocks of Wheeler Geologic Area were deposited during violent volcanic activity approximately 30 million years ago.

A remote arch frames a portion of Colorado's spectacular canyon country along the Western Slope.

Lion House is an unrestored Anasazi ruin located deep inside
the Ute Mountain Tribal Park in southwest Colorado.

Impressive hoodoos approaching sixty feet in height stand
undisturbed in a little known region of western Colorado.

While not as large or spectacular as the Great Sand Dunes, the North Sand Hills near Walden have an enchanting beauty of their own.

Steady winds in North Park have etched intricate patterns into the North Sand Hills.

A large granite arch with a horizontal span of seventy feet
stands high atop a hillside near the town of Leadville.

The late afternoon sun is reflected in the shallow, rocky waters of Emma Lake along the Tenmile Range.

Limestone formations known as stalactites, stalagmites, and cave bacon fill a large room called The Barn in Glenwood Caverns.

King's Row in Glenwood Caverns has the highest concentration
of stalactites and stalagmites of any cave room in Colorado.

The Medicine Bow Mountains, shown here reflected in Meadow Creek Reservoir, are one of the least-visited ranges in Colorado.

A tributary of the Animas River creates a dramatic waterfall as it descends from the high peaks of the San Juan Mountains.

A high alpine pond reflects spectacular Rocky Mountain
scenery along Paradise Divide in the Elk Mountains.

A solitary butte rises above the grasslands of the Great Plains
near Purgatoire Canyon in southeastern Colorado.

Over millions of years, the Dolores River in southwestern Colorado has carved out the 2,000-foot-deep Dolores River Canyon.

A large natural arch known as La Ventana is illuminated
by the first light of day in southern Colorado.

Lowry Pueblo is one of the most impressive Anasazi ruins in the recently-created Canyons of the Ancients National Monument.

Colorful, mushroom-shaped rocks rise towards the sky
in a seldom-visited region of eastern Colorado.

An imposing sandstone fin known as Castle Rock rises
above a flat, arid landscape in far western Colorado.

A large butte rises above a field of purple and yellow wildflowers
in an unpopulated portion of northwest Colorado.

The Rio Grande River reflects the late afternoon light
as it flows towards the New Mexico border.

The Gates of Lodore provide a dramatic, but foreboding entryway into the canyons of Dinosaur National Monument.

An ancient Anasazi ruin constructed around 1000 A.D. stands largely undisturbed in a remote alcove in southwest Colorado.

A natural arch known as Window Rock sits high above
a canyon south of the town of Cripple Creek.

A large sandstone arch frames a distant hoodoo
along Colorado's Western Slope.

The Yampa River winds through dramatic canyon country in Dinosaur National Monument before merging with the Green River.

A small window in a long-abandoned building frames
a mountain peak along Colorado's Front Range.

The afternoon sun peaks through a bristlecone pine
on the side of the 14,000-foot Mount Bross.

A spectacular sunset lights up the sky over West Butte in Pawnee National Grasslands.

An intriguing landscape of red rock formations is highlighted
by a large spire in a valley near Cañon City.

An impressive waterfall weaves its way down a mountainside in the rugged San Juan Mountains.

The Cache la Poudre River flows along red and
black banded walls west of Fort Collins.

A natural arch is immersed in afternoon shadows
in a secluded canyon in western Colorado.

The Rio Grande River begins its descent into a gradually deepening canyon near the New Mexico border.

The Green River flows through Browns Park National Wildlife Refuge, a haven for geese, ducks, and other migrating birds.

A dramatic formation known as Needle Rock rises
800 feet into the air near the town of Crawford.

A small hoodoo in western Colorado bears a remarkable resemblance to the stone statues of Easter Island.

A small arch frames a distant mesa in an isolated
and little known region of western Colorado.

A massive granite cliff rises above Unaweep Canyon
near the town of Gateway in western Colorado.

Enormous sandstone walls are reflected in the Green River, just south of its confluence with the Yampa River in Dinosaur National Monument.

The first light of day illuminates the 14,000-foot
Crestone Needle above South Colony Lake.

A high alpine pond along Paradise Divide reflects the
peaks of the Ruby Range shortly after sunrise.

Sunflowers and purple daisies cover a field as far as the
eye can see in Mayflower Gulch, near Leadville.

The bell-shaped East Butte, which served as a landmark to early
pioneers, rises above the grasslands of the eastern plains.

Castlewood Canyon State Park, near Franktown, comes alive with color in mid-October, as the vegetation embraces for winter.

A diminutive cloud floats past one of Colorado's most spectacular, but least-known natural arches.

A small, but picturesque waterfall flows beneath the
14,000-foot Quandary Peak in Summit County.

White sandstone rocks deposited by an ancient riverbed sit atop colorful clay deposits in the eastern plains of Colorado.

A large column surrounded by several stalactites is just one of
many fascinating formations found in Cave of the Winds.

Although Cave of the Winds is currently a popular attraction, it took
a chance discovery in 1880 to uncover this hidden wonder.

An impressive sandstone arch stands hidden atop
a rocky cliff face along Colorado's Western Slope.

Abandoned structures around the old Boston Mine have had varying success in holding up against the elements.

An ancient Chacoan structure called the Great House sits high atop a mesa in Chimney Rock Archaeological Area in southern Colorado.

Dome Rock, located north of Cripple Creek, is reminiscent
of the much more famous Half Dome in Yosemite.

The multicolored hills and badlands around Vermillion Creek
in far northwest Colorado are seldom visited by humans.

Immense trunks of 34 million-year-old petrified Sequoia trees
are found in Florissant Fossil Beds National Monument.

A large hoodoo composed of rocks and compacted dirt
rises skyward in an isolated part of western Colorado.

Thimble Rock is framed in the window of a long-abandoned building known as Driggs Mansion in Unaweep Canyon.

Dramatic storm clouds pass over a wonderland of purple,
orange, and white rocks in eastern Colorado..

Otherworldly scenes unfold around every corner in the
multicolored badlands on the eastern plains.

Late afternoon shadows fall upon a large, but little-known arch along Colorado's Front Range.

Cascading waters stream down a rocky cliff face
high in Colorado's San Juan Mountains.

The dramatic peaks of the Gore Range are reflected
in the still waters of Piney Lake, north of Vail.

Egg-shaped volcanic rocks make up a portion of Wheeler
Geologic Area near the town of Creede.

Wheeler Mountain is reflected in the ice-covered Blue
Lake on a spring afternoon in Summit County.

Dramatic cloud formations surround Chimney Rock
along Owl Creek Pass in the Cimarron Mountains.

Wildflowers cover the valley floor below a picturesque waterfall high above Silverton in the San Juan Mountains.

A small, unnamed arch sits undisturbed along
the Dolores River in southwest Colorado.

An ancient bristlecone pine clings tenaciously to existence amidst the harsh elements on Mount Bross.

The doorway of a long-abandoned structure now leads into Chinns Lake in Clear Creek County.

Peru Creek descends rapidly from its headwaters below
Mount Edwards near the town of Montezuma..

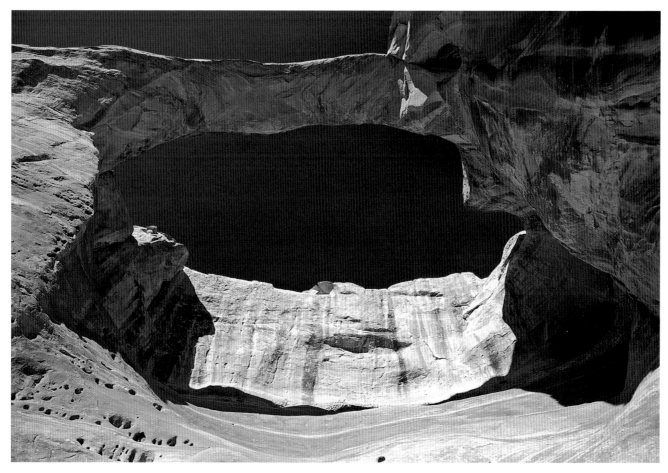

A huge pothole arch was carved out by the slow, but steady erosive forces of water in western Colorado.

An ancient stone tower built by the Anasazi Indians around 1200 A.D. remains standing in a seldom-visited region of western Colorado.

Prehistoric Anasazi structures have withstood the ravages of time atop Lion Canyon in the Ute Mountain Tribal Park.

Bizarre rock formations are illuminated by the late
afternoon sun along Colorado's Western Slope.

Slater Creek flows below Long Mountain on an
expansive ranch near the Wyoming border.

The Flat Tops are reflected in Trappers Lake in White
River National Forest in northern Colorado.

Massive rock pillars rise above a stand of aspen along
Owl Creek Pass in the Cimarron Mountains.

A small arch in San Juan National Forest frames an aspen grove during the height of fall color in Colorado.

A volcanic formation known as Needle Rock rises
high above rural farmland in western Colorado.

An arch inside Devils Backbone Open Space
frames a portion of Colorado's Front Range.

A high-altitude beaver pond in Summit County reflects
Ruby Mountain on a summer afternoon.

Several stalactites, which have formed over thousands of years, fill a subterranean chamber in Glenwood Caverns.

# Acknowledgments

I would like to thank Nat Coalson, who provided invaluable digital assistance on this book, as well as Dax Oliver and Catamount Mayhugh, who gave me feedback on portions of the text.